THE TEACHING OF
THE CHURCH REGARDING
BAPTISM

Karl Barth

THE TEACHING OF
THE CHURCH REGARDING
BAPTISM

TRANSLATED BY
ERNEST A PAYNE

———

Wipf & Stock
PUBLISHERS
Eugene, Oregon

Wipf and Stock Publishers
199 W 8th Ave, Suite 3
Eugene, OR 97401

The Teaching of the Church Regarding Baptism
By Barth, Karl
Copyright©1948 Theologischer Verlag Zurich
ISBN: 1-59752-799-8
Publication date 6/23/2006
Previously published by SCM Press, 1948

Copyright©1943 of the German original version
Theologischer Verlag Zurich

TRANSLATOR'S PREFACE

BOTH the theology and the practice of the Church in regard to baptism are today the subject of searching thought and discussion in many different Christian traditions. Communions which practise infant-baptism, as well as those which, since the Reformation, have stood for the baptism of believers only, are alike compelled to re-examine their doctrine of the Church and the sacraments. On these matters, as on so many others, the Swiss theologians, and in particular Dr. Barth and Dr. Brunner, have important things to say to the English-speaking world as well as to their own. Professor Emil Brunner discussed baptism in the last chapter of *Wahrheit als Begegnung* (available for English readers as *The Divine-Human Encounter*, S.C.M. Press, 1944).

A quarter of a century ago Dr. Barth in his commentary on the Epistle to the Romans wrote as follows :—

"Baptism is a sacrament of truth and holiness; and it is a sacrament, because it is the sign which directs us to God's revelation of eternal life and declares, not merely the Christian 'myth,' but—the Word of God. It does not merely signify eternal reality, but is eternal reality, because it points significantly beyond its own concreteness. Baptism mediates the new creation : it is not itself grace, but from first to

5

last a means of grace. As the question which men put to God is always also His answer to it; as human faith is enclosed invisibly by the faithfulness of God; so also the human act of baptism is enclosed by that action of God on behalf of men which it declares " (E.T., p. 192).

Since then Dr. Barth has developed and systematized the prophetic insights which have made him one of the most stimulating and influential thinkers of our time. He is engaged upon the exposition of a comprehensive Christian dogmatic which will treat in due place of the doctrine of the Church. In the meantime, however, the lecture which follows makes a particular and distinctive contribution to the current discussion of baptism and shows the conclusions to which Dr. Barth has been led by his study of the New Testament. The lecture was delivered to a gathering of Swiss theological students on 7 May, 1943, at Gwatt am Thunersee and was subsequently printed under the title *Die Kirchliche Lehre von der Taufe* as No. 14 of the series of *Theologische Studien*, edited by Dr. Barth himself and published by the Evangelischer Verlag A. G. Zollikon—Zürich.

I am grateful to my friends, the Rev. and Mrs. Kurt Emmerich, who first called my attention to the pamphlet and helped to secure Dr. Barth's permission for this translation. I am very conscious that I have not overcome all the difficulties or avoided all the pitfalls which beset the translator. They are formidable indeed in the case of a theologian of Dr. Barth's calibre, and with such a subject. How shall *Bild, Abbild, Darstellung, Zeichen*, etc., be adequately rendered and distinguished in English? My translation, which is from the second edition, would not have reached its present form but for the co-operation of others. Dr. Hugh Martin and the S.C.M. Press Board encouraged me to essay the task when others, more competent than I, drew back. Dr. P. W. Evans gave me encouragement and help on a number of different occasions. Miss Joyce Booth typed my manuscript. Dr. and Mrs. A. B. Crabtree generously and carefully read the typescript and made a number of valuable suggestions. However many the blemishes that remain, I hope it will be clear to every reader that Dr. Barth has things to say to which all those concerned for a true doctrine and practice of baptism should give heed.

ERNEST A. PAYNE

Regent's Park College,
   Oxford.

THE TEACHING OF
THE CHURCH REGARDING
BAPTISM

I

CHRISTIAN baptism is in essence the representation *(Abbild)* of a man's renewal through his participation by means of the power of the Holy Spirit in the death and resurrection of Jesus Christ, and therewith the representation of man's association with Christ, with the covenant of grace which is concluded and realised in Him, and with the fellowship of His Church.

The Greek word βαπτίζειν and the German word *taufen* (from *Tiefe*, depth) originally and properly describe the process by which a man or an object is completely immersed in water and then withdrawn from it again. Primitive baptism carried out in this manner had in its mode, exactly like the circumcision of the Old Testament, the character of a direct threat to life, succeeded immediately by the corresponding deliverance and preservation, the raising from baptism[1]. One can hardly deny that baptism carried out as immersion—as it was in the West until well on into the Middle Ages—showed what was represented in far more expressive fashion than did

---

[1] Cf. the German phrase " ein kind aus der Taufe heben "—
to be godfather or godmother to a child. E.A.P.

the affusion which later became customary, especially when this affusion was reduced from a real wetting to a sprinkling and eventually in practice to a mere moistening with as little water as possible. Who would think that Paul, according to 1 Cor. x. 1 ff., saw the prefiguration of baptism in so critical an experience as the passage of the Israelites through the Red Sea? One may surely agree with Luther[1] that it would be well to give so complete and pregnant an affair its full and complete expression: *sicut et institutum est sine dubio a Christo.* Is the last word on the matter to be, that facility of administration, health and propriety are important reasons for doing otherwise?[2] Or will a Christianity return whose more vigorous imagination will be satisfied no longer with the innocuous form of present-day baptism any more than with certain other inoffensive features of modern Christianity?

Luther, however, did not regard the original form of baptism as necessary to salvation. He was therefore opposed to all those who wished to make this an actual article of faith *(Glaubensfrage)*, on the well-founded ground, first, that βαπτίζειν signifies historically *aspergere*, affusion, wetting—though a really efficacious wetting. Further, in regard to certain of the New Testament narratives (e.g. the baptism of the three thousand at Pentecost) it is questionable what outward form of baptism is in mind. Moreover, it is certain that soon after the time of the apostles, at all events in the case of the baptism of the sick (the so-called *baptismus clinicorum*), the original rule was broken from time to time. These considerations, however, do not alter the fact

[1] *De capt. Babyl.*
[2] Cf. B. Bartmann, *Lehrbuch d. Dogm.* II, 1920, p. 258

that it is impossible to understand the meaning of baptism, unless one keeps in mind that it implies a threat of death and a deliverance to life; nor that, generally speaking, the custom followed in baptism is to be called good or bad as it more or less adequately represents such a process.

What baptism portrays, according to the basic passage in Romans vi. lf., is a supremely critical happening,—a real event whose light and shade fall upon the candidate in the course of his baptism. This happening is his participation in the death and resurrection of Jesus Christ: that is, the fact that at a particular time and place, in the year A.D. 30 outside Jerusalem on the cross at Golgotha, not Jesus Christ alone, but with Him also this particular individual died eternally, and that, in the garden of Joseph of Arimathea, not Jesus Christ alone, but with Him also this particular individual rose from the dead for evermore. Not only his sins and he not only in his character as sinner—but really he himself as subject, met his death then and there, was then and there buried, so that, although he is still in existence, he is in effect now no more. And not only did God's grace begin for him then and there, but also his real life in God's eternal Kingdom and therefore in its glory; so that he can now no more die, but can only live, even though he will one day die. Therefore, according to Romans vi. he is now dead to sin, but has become alive unto God for an existence in His service.

This is what happens for him and to him in the death and resurrection of Jesus Christ; in very truth for him and to him, in the power of the Holy Spirit which is poured out upon him. For it is the Holy Spirit, proceeding from Jesus Christ and moving this particular man, which unites him to Jesus Christ like a body to its head, making him belong to Jesus Christ and making everything that Jesus Christ is and does belong to him. This happens in such a manner that he can no more be without Jesus Christ because Jesus Christ can no more be without him; he is no more outside but in Jesus Christ and with Him to the end of all things, standing with Him at the dawn of a new heaven and a new earth. " Wherefore if any man is in Christ, he is a new creature : the old things are passed away : behold, they are become new " (2 Cor. v. 17).

As the Holy Spirit is the agent of this union of man with Jesus Christ, therefore the work of the Holy Spirit belongs inseparably to the death and resurrection of Jesus Christ and to the happening portrayed in baptism. As the Holy Spirit is the agent of this union, what happens is " baptism with the Holy Spirit " and it is so described by all four gospels and by the Acts of the Apostles, to distinguish it from water baptism as such. Thus it is that water baptism is the μυστήριον ἀναγεννήσεως,[1] the *sacramentum regenerationis*. What befalls a man in that participation in the death and resurrection of Jesus Christ through the work of the Holy Spirit, which is set forth in baptism, is indeed his rebirth to new life in the Age to Come. It is accomplished through his full justification before God, through the full forgiveness of his sins, through his full consecration to God's service.

The Reformed theology of the 17th century meant and said nothing other than this when, in accordance with its central point of view, it[2] described this reality

[1] Gregory of Nyssa, *Or. Cat.,* **33**

[2] Z. B. Polan, *Synt. Theol. chr.* 1609, col. 3185

12

as the admission of a man to the *foedus gratiae Dei*, which was established by God's eternal decree of election in Jesus Christ and which was realised in time in the coming, the death and the resurrection of the same Jesus Christ. As a partner in this covenant and therefore a brother of Jesus Christ, man is born again as a child of God and a citizen of the new Age. He is moreover righteous before God, because declared free from his sins and therefore consecrated to Him. These things a man becomes because he believes in Jesus Christ and in his own renewal as a child of God through Him, and because he confesses this his faith, becoming by reason of his confession a responsible partner in the divine grace, a living member of the Church of Jesus Christ. All this— that is, everything accomplished in the death and the resurrection of Jesus Christ, right up to and including the last thing of all, namely, the praise of God which breaks from the lips of the forgiven sinner and is accepted by grace—is the reality which is por-· trayed in water-baptism.

According to John i, the water baptism of John witnesses to the baptism of the Spirit which is to be directly accomplished by Jesus Christ Himself. According to the foundation passage Romans vi. 5, it is the ὁμοίωμα (likeness) of His death. Therefore and in this sense we call baptism a representation *(Abbild)*. We might instead call it a seal (σφραγίς), following a usage which was widespread in the second century, or a sign *(signum)*, according to the terminology of Augustine which later came to prevail. So far as I know, there is no teaching about Christian baptism which would directly contest the view that water baptism itself is also, and indeed primarily, to be understood as a symbol, that is, as a type *(Entsprechung)* and a representation *(Darstellung)*, or, according to Gregory of Nyssa, a copy μίμησις —of that other divine-human reality which it attests. One can obscure this by expressions which appear stronger or more definite, but one cannot contest it.

Baptism is holy and hallowing, though we have yet to see why and how far. But it is neither God, nor Jesus Christ, nor the covenant, nor grace, nor faith, nor the Church. It bears witness to all these as the event in which God in Jesus Christ makes a man His child and a member of His covenant, awakening faith through His grace and calling a man to life in the Church. Baptism testifies to a man that this event is not his fancy but is objective reality which no power on earth can alter and which God has pledged Himself to maintain in all circumstances. It testifies to him that God has directed all His words and works towards him and does not cease so to do. It testifies to him what has already been declared in the *signum audibile* of the word of Christian teaching and instruction, and has already come to pass in fact after the latter, because it occurs also at his baptism and will occur again after his baptism. It testifies this to him, however, as *signum visibile:* as the speaking likeness of that threat of death and deliverance to life, in the midst of which he is concerned with no one but himself as the one who is threatened and delivered; in which also he is not only dealt with but, by yielding himself to this threat and deliverance, finds himself taking an active part. Baptism then is a picture in which, man, it is true, is not the most important figure but is certainly the second most important.

[1] *Or. cat.,* 85

This is the essence of baptism : to be this picture, this witness and sign. That it is only a picture is evident, apart from anything else, from the inadequacy with which the threat and deliverance—ultimately harmless even in the most pointed form of the representation—correspond to the actual death and actual eternal life of man, with which it deals objectively.

What John i, 8 says of John the Baptist : " He was not the light but came that he might bear witness of the light "; what the Baptist according to John i, 20, iii, 28, so confessed of himself : " I am not the Christ," and Jesus conversely said of Himself : " The witness which I have is greater than that of John " (John v, 36); all this holds good also of baptism and points to a limiting principle which in a sound doctrine of baptism must be neither put on one side nor rendered ineffective. One does no honour to baptism by interpreting it as if it were in its essence more than the representation of the sacred history *(Heilsgeschichte)* which comes to pass between God and man in Jesus Christ. It has its full honour precisely in being in fact the most living and expressive picture of that history : the visible sign of the invisible *nativitas spiritualis* at the entrance gate of the Church and at the beginning of every Christian life.

II.

THE power or potency *(Kraft)* of baptism consists in this—that as an element in the Church's message it is a free word and deed of Jesus Christ Himself.

Baptism is no dead or dumb representation, but a living and expressive one. Its potency lies in the fact that it comprehends the whole movement of sacred history *(Heilsgeschichte)* and that it is therefore *res potentissima et efficacissima.* All that it intends and actually effects is the result of this potency. It exercises its power as it shows to a man that objective reality to which he himself belongs (and of which it is a sign) in such a way that he can only forget or miss it *per nefas;* in such a way, at all events, that he becomes by its marks himself a marked man, by its portraiture one who is himself portrayed. We next ask therefore : whence comes this potency?

We begin from the fact that baptism is in any case a part of the Church's proclamation and that it is plainly a human act. Like the Lord's Supper, preaching, prayer, the whole worship of the Church, pastoral care, works of charity, church order and Christian education, it is a part of the Church's proclamation. One is accustomed to distinguish it from the other activities of the Church as, like the Lord's Supper, a " sacrament." But whilst being clear about baptism and the Lord's Supper, it is even more important to realise that all the activities of the Church are in their way sacramental. That is to say, they are activities involving signs and symbols ; moreover, they are dependent for their effectiveness on certain fixed signs and symbols. Baptism (as we have said) is in any case, like all the Church's acts, plainly a human act. If in fact it has the potency of a living and expressive representation, able to represent and denote man, then it owes this to the fact that it is, together with all the other parts of the Church's proclamation, in itself and in its complete humanity, still indirectly and mediately a free word and act of Jesus Christ Himself. It is this which gives life to all parts of the Church's proclamation and to baptism along with the others. The Church stands under the government of her Lord, an instrument at His disposal. When she expresses herself in human words and deeds, she lays hold of the promise that whoever listens to her listens to Him. The Church did not found or gather herself. She was founded and gathered by her Lord and so she continues to be. Similarly, the Church did not herself invent the different parts of her proclamation; nor did she invent baptism. She administers it as instituted by her Lord. She obeys His command. By word and deed she serves those who are His, in hope and expectation that through the power of her words and deeds His word and His deed will find expression.

The water-baptism of John witnesses to the baptism with Spirit and fire of Jesus Christ Himself. For that very reason, the mighty dispenser of water-baptism is neither John, nor the Church—but the Lord Jesus Christ Himself, though indirectly and mediately, it is effected through the service of John and through the service of the Church. Who else but Jesus Christ Himself could effectively testify of Jesus Christ? As Luther rightly and repeatedly made clear in his sermons on Matt. iii, 13f. (following Chrysostom, Ambrose, Thomas Aquinas and Bonaventura) and Calvin also believed,[1] it is the Lord who makes water-baptism powerful for repentance and the forgiveness of sins. He, who needed not these things, submitted Himself to them, thereby setting forth both what happened on Golgotha and also what happened on Easter morning, thus declaring

[1] *Institutes* IV, 15, 6

His solidarity with sinners. Baptism was thereby made a living and expressive representation of Christ's high-priestly death and resurrection. Whoever now is baptized may expect like Him to see the heavens opened, to hear the voice of the Father, and to share in the Holy Spirit. Therefore it is called, and indeed is, baptism in the name of the Father, the Son and the Holy Spirit. The covenant of grace was to be established through Christ's death and revealed in His resurrection. By thus putting Himself already into the representation that pre-figured these things (and afterwards into their mirroring), Jesus Christ "instituted" *(eingesetzt)* baptism.

All the other passages which occur to one at this point—for example, Matt. xxviii, 19—are to be understood as the ratification and enforcement of this actual "institution" of baptism. By this testimony to the service He was to render—by thus witnessing to Himself as the Suffering Servant of Isaiah liii and the Lamb of God who bears the sins of the world (John i, 29f. Cf. Mark x, 38, Luke xii, 50)—Christ made Himself Lord of baptism. He Who, in every baptism which is properly administered in the services of the Church, is the Chief Character, the primary and true Baptizer, thus turned baptism into something powerful, living and expressive. Baptism is the acted parable of His death, in which (according to Romans vi, 5) man is at his own baptism "planted." It is a repetition of Christ's baptism, in which man himself as the candidate for baptism is now the second most important figure. To quote Luther once more, baptism is "God's Word in water" *(Larger Catechism)*, that is, Jesus Christ Himself is the first to be dealt with in this act and to take an active part in it. By His

18

own participation in it, He gave command and commission. Therein lies the potency of baptism.

Though it is Christ's institution of it, His word and deed, which gives potency to baptism, it must of course be emphasized that it is His *free* word and deed. He Who, when He let Himself be baptized by John in Jordan, prefigured and represented Himself as the servant of all those who baptize and are baptized in His name and that of the Father and the Spirit, thereby showed Himself as also their sovereign Lord and the sole and powerful head of the Church. The potency of baptism depends upon Christ who is the chief actor in it. It has no independent potency in itself. Nor have any other of the parts of the Church's proclamation. Though the Church utters the Word in baptism and performs the act, what must always be believed in, loved, expected and prayed for is the power of His free Person, sent down for this very purpose. It cannot be manipulated by men. It is always power which Christ Himself personally and freely grants. It is something promised which He Himself alone can provide.

At this point certain qualifications are necessary. All those are right who have drawn attention to the fact that there is a genuine symbolic power in the water itself and who have therefore spoken of its use being necessary in baptism. Tertullian[1] and Ambrose[2] point back to the movement of the Spirit of God over the waters at the time of the creation. It is certainly permissible for us to ascribe a certain saving significance to our douche of cold water on the morning of each new day. But one must not press such symbolism too far. The natural sym-

[1] *De bapt.* 4   [2] *De myst.* 3, 8

bolism of water and its ordinary use can point in every other possible direction, as well as to the death and resurrection of Jesus, the events upon which man's regeneration depends. Such general symbolism can entirely fail. For anything to be a witness or a sign the necessary power must be present. Water and its use must first receive their special meaning. And they do not receive it because of anything given or attributed to them in a certain way by the Church. They receive it because Jesus Christ is Lord of Nature and because He has of His own free will allowed them to serve His word and work. As Luther in the *Shorter Catechism* puts it : " Truly water cannot do it, but the Word of God which is with and on the water, and the faith which believes such Word of God in the water. For without the Word of God the water is simple water, and not baptism; but with the Word of God it is baptism."

Zwingli would have been right had he been content to say that baptism is a symbol of the faith of the Church and of the faith of her individual members, and that its performance is an act of remembrance and therefore an act of confession, and therefore something confirming such faith. How should Jesus Christ demonstrate the power of baptism, if not for faith and in the faith both of the Church and the baptized? Unfortunately Zwingli wanted to say something else; namely, that the potency of baptism is now limited to the power of a faith which strengthens itself by the use of the symbol. To this it must be said that the power of faith is not something dependent on itself—a power which may indeed strengthen itself in pious ceremonies—but that it is the power of the one exercising it and really nothing else; and that even this, and this by itself, and also the power of Jesus Christ, are really the same as the power of baptism. But the power of baptism really lies precisely here—that it shows like a clear mirror that the Church and those baptized within her are not left alone with their own faith, are not dependent on themselves, but that faith has its ground and essence in the objective reality of the divine covenant of grace.

The tradition of the Church of Rome, in its turn, would be right if it is said that the potency of baptism is the potency of the *opus operatum* of Jesus Christ, the potency of His reconciling work wrought once for all, and ever and again made effective through the free might of the Holy Spirit. Unfortunately this is not what is said. Instead, there is talk of an *opus operatum* of the correctly administered baptismal rite, which becomes powerful and effectual by its own means, just as faith does in the teaching of Zwingli. To this it must be said that the potency of baptism cannot be a potency dependent on itself or one which itself produces its effects. We read in Acts viii, 14f. concerning the Samaritans that those who had (unlike the disciples of John in Acts xix, lf.) heard the mighty preaching of Philip were baptized expressly in the name of the Lord Jesus, and yet that they had not received the Holy Spirit. Is not this passage (together with Acts xix) an explicit warning against any view which would ascribe to the baptismal water, the ecclesiastical rite, or the parts of the Church's proclamation in general, their own even relatively independent power of action over against the free enactment of the Lord? In 1 Cor. vi, 11 it does not say that we are washed, sanctified and justified in baptism, but "in the name of the Lord Jesus Christ and in the Spirit of our God." If baptism is a true witness, that means that it is living and expressive not in its own power, but in the power of Him to whom it bears witness and by whose command it is carried out.

Likewise, Luther and the older Lutherans would have been right had they been content, in opposition to all Separatism and Spiritualism *(allem unkirch-lichen Spiritualismus)*, to direct attention to the orderly inter-relation of sign and substance, of representation and reality and, therefore, of Baptism and Spirit, of Water and the Word of God. Luther spoke truly concerning baptism so long as he simply hammered at the idea that it is God's Word or Command which is the "kernel in the water" *(Kern im Wasser)*. But with characteristic exaggeration in that same *Larger Catechism*, he goes farther in this matter, as with his teaching on the Lord's Supper. Of the baptismal water itself he says that it is " comprised in God's word and commandment and thereby sanctified "; he calls it " God's water," a " divine, heavenly, holy and blessed water " and asserts that faith " clings " to this water. Later he is able to say that it is " such water as takes away sin, death and all misery and helps us to heaven and eternal life. Such a precious sweetened water, *Aromaticum* and medicine comes into existence because God is Himself intermingled with it. But God is a God of life. Since He is now in this water, therefore it must be the true *Aqua vitae*, which drives away death and hell and gives immortality."[1] And the older Lutherans did not omit to systematize this exaggeration by their teaching that the *efficacia* of baptism is *coniunctim* that of the Holy Spirit and that of the water consecrated

[1] *Weimar Ausgabe* 52, 102

22

by the repetition of the words of institution. We can follow this teaching as little as we follow the Zwinglian and the Roman. Divine-human power and some other, such as that of water-baptism, can neither be distinguished as two effective factors working on the same plane, nor as such can they be allowed to meet, without making it uncertain on whom or what in such a mixture *(Mischgestalt)* one should believe. To believe in Jesus Christ *and* in water consecrated by His presence is a dangerous thing and is not confirmed by any necessary relationship between the two.

These are some of the qualifications which have here to be borne in mind. The promise of the potency of baptism is apprehended with confidence and certainty precisely in so far as its fulfilment is expected solely through the free enactment of Jesus Christ.

Something must be said about an important consequence which follows from this. The power of Jesus Christ, which is the only power in baptism, is not dependent upon the carrying out of baptism. Baptism has the necessity of a command which cannot fail to be heard *(necessitas praecepti)*. It has not the necessity of an indispensable medium *(necessitas medii)*. The free word and work of Christ can make use of other means. That the Church is commanded to use this means cannot signify that Jesus Christ Himself is limited to it. The domain of the divine covenant of grace is larger than the domain of the Church, Christ's *regnum* wider than His *ecclesia*.[1] The rule for us is that outside the Church there is no salvation, but the Lord of the Church is not limited thereto. The

[1] Cf. O. Cullmann, *Königsherrschaft Christi und Kirche im Neuen Testament,* 1941

remark about water and Spirit in John iii, 5 has not this in view. Mark xvi, 16 to be sure says : " He that believeth and is baptized shall be saved," but then simply " He that disbelieveth shall be condemned." The representatives of the view that baptism is an absolute necessity for salvation, therefore, in their dogmatic works, always taught with a certain hesitancy that this threat must cover the absence of baptism. At least for the unbaptized children of Christians, almost the whole church has held out at all times the prospect of either a friendly exception or a somewhat modified perdition (the so-called *limbus infantium*). Further, Roman dogmatic speaks of the martyrs' blood-baptism *(baptismus sanguinis)* as sufficiently taking the place of water-baptism; while since the famous funeral sermon of Ambrose for the Emperor Valentinian II, who died while a catechumen, it has spoken also of a baptism of desire in cases of perfect love and repentance *(bapt. flaminis)*. In the Middle Ages, under certain conditions, even entry into a monastic order availed in place of baptism. But casuistry of this kind— which is both miserable and ambiguous—is surely completely superfluous for the solution of the problem before us. It was much more to the point when Luther in his early years, preaching in lively and happy fashion, declared : " A man may believe even if he is not baptized; for baptism is no more than an outward sign that the divine promise ought to admonish us. If a man can have it, it is good, let him take it; for no one ought to despise it. But if a man cannot have it, or is refused it, he is not condemned, so long as he believes the Gospel. For where

[1] *Weimar Ausgabe,* 10, 111, 142
[2] *Institutes* IV, 15, 20

the Gospel is, there is baptism and all else that a Christian man needs."[1] Calvin[2] also explicitly declared that a man cannot be deprived of renewing grace if he dies before baptism; certainly therefore we must not think of the operations of the covenant of grace as being in any sense dependent on the sign which seals it. The classic Protestant dogmatic of both Confessions—whilst it abandoned teaching about this or that particular aspect of baptism— was rightly united in the view that the Church and Christendom must hold to the command of the Lord and to His promise, even though (as Augustine[1] had already expressed it) being deprived of baptism as such cannot condemn a man or shut him out of the Kingdom of Heaven. That can only come from the slighting or despising of baptism. Plainly, the power of baptism is not limited to water-baptism. There is no need which makes necessary baptism at the point of death (the so-called *Nottaufen*). It would not be true but untrue—certainly in relation to water-baptism—to assert the contrary.

III.

THE meaning and intention *(Sinn)* of baptism is the glorifying of God in the building up of the Church of Jesus Christ through the pledge given to a man, with divine certainty, of grace directed towards him, and through the pledge of allegiance pronounced over a man, with divine authority, with reference to the grateful service which is required of him.

[1] *De civ. Dei,* XIII, 7

We turn now to the question as to what happens in baptism to correspond to its nature and potency. What can and ought to be effected in and through this rite separating it from any casual, arbitrary or meaningless action? What is its special work, distinguishing it from certain other actions which are in themselves meaning-full? What is meant when Titus iii, 5 describes baptism as "the washing of regeneration and renewing of the Holy Ghost" or when the *Nic. Const.* refers to "baptism for the forgiving of sins?" Here also we must take care neither to separate what is really now one, nor to confuse what is not one.

In view of the points established regarding the nature and potency of baptism, manifestly one cannot properly maintain what would be here asserted by Roman and Lutheran and Anglican baptismal teaching : namely, that water-baptism conferred by the Church is *as such* a causative or generative means by which there are imparted to man the forgiveness of sins, the Holy Spirit and even faith— a means by which grace is poured out upon him, so that he is saved and made blessed—a means by which his rebirth is effected, by which he is taken into the covenant of the grace of God and incorporated in the Church. Later Lutherans have described baptism as the introduction "of a divine and living spark of Christian life" into the consciousness and will of the baptized,[1] as "the introduction into the old man of a new, spiritual germ from the redemptive fulness of Christ."[2] Here there takes place a confounding of the subjects, that is, on the one side Jesus Christ and on the other the one who is in His name carry-

---

[1] A. F. C. Vilmar, *Dogmatik* 1874, II, p. 244

[2] F. H. R. Frank, *Syst. d. chr. Wahrheit*, II, 1886, p. 272

ing out the Church's baptism—a hazardous move at least. Here in any case that which is the special characteristic of the baptismal experience, and its peculiarity in relation to what it represents, is obliterated, in a fashion which certainly cannot be shown to be the case with the New Testament passages which are cited in support of this view (e.g., Gal. iii, 27; Rom. vi. 4; 1 Peter iii, 21; Eph. v, 26; Titus iii, 5f; Acts ii, 38). Let us remember that baptism is the representation, the seal, the sign, the copy, the symbol of our redemption. And let us remember that the power of baptism lies in the free word and deed of Jesus Christ. Our baptism is no more the cause of our redemption than is our faith. " Is then the outward bathing the washing away of sins? No; only the blood of Jesus Christ and the Holy Ghost cleanses us from all sin."[1] In baptism we have to do not with the *causa* but with the *cognitio salutis.*[2] If one confounds *causa* and *cognitio,* at once and inevitably one overlooks and mistakes the peculiarity of the purpose which baptism serves (and also that of faith!).

One must, however, in justice grant to the realism of the Roman, Lutheran and Anglican teaching regarding baptism that it is a warning, which is in line with the New Testament passages cited, not to overlook the special work of baptism and not to deny it from fear of the danger of magic. It is a work which in its special character is auxiliary, but this is its special function. The Heidelberg Catechism, also, is right when it declares (Question 73) that the Holy Spirit calls baptism the laver of regeneration and the washing away of sins " not

[1] *Heidelberg Catechism,* 72
[2] Calvin, *Institutes* IV, 15, 2

without good reason." The sacrament does not redeem—since under redemption the experience of reconciliation, rebirth and deliverance into faith must be understood. But the word and work of Jesus Christ, which in this sense are alone redemptive, and faith in Him, have also a sacramental dimension and form *(Gestalt)*. It is beçause this is absent from Zwingli that his baptismal teaching—like that regarding the Lord's Supper—is so strangely flat and cold, and só unsatisfactory in relation to the New Testament references. The word and work of Christ, alone redemptive, extend not only to faith but also *ad fidei nostrae sensum*[1]; for even faith itself implies decision and experience. In baptism (as in the Lord's Supper, in preaching and in every part of the Church's proclamation) the word and work of Jesus Christ are a gift of salvation which is recognised—a revelation of the covenant of grace, of rebirth, of the forgiveness of sins, which satisfies —a confirmation to the believing man of the complete divine-human reality which supports and surrounds him—a summons to the believing man, engaging him to respond to this reality in his own being and to become obedient to the Holy Spirit according to the gift that is his.

The word and work of Jesus Christ is not only powerful in itself; it is that which attracts our apperception by its powerful representation of itself. Whilst it alone is the generative cause of salvation, it desires to be seen, heard, perceived, savoured, understood, considered, and obeyed, by the man who is saved and believes in his salvation. In the most comprehensive manner it wants to be recognised and experienced. It is not a matter of course that this

[1] Calvin, *Institutes* IV 15, 15

should happen. It really is not a matter of course that reality becomes truth for us. We cannot ourselves ensure it. Reality itself, the Lord Jesus Christ Himself, must give this to us. Therefore Calvin and other teachers of the old Reformed Church spoke, rightly and with emphasis, not only of a *significare, declarare, repraesentare, offerre*, but also of an *exhibere* and *conferre* which take place in baptism, and on man's side of an *accipere, obtinere, impetrare.* The sacramental happening in which a real gift comes to man from Jesus Christ Himself is not in fact any less genuine a happening, because Christ's word and work on this occasion in this dimension and form, and Christ's power on this occasion, have not a causative or generative, but a cognitive aim.

According to 1 Peter iii, 21, baptism is not " the putting away of the filth of the flesh "—that happens on quite another plane—but " the appeal of a good conscience toward God, through the resurrection of Jesus Christ." In the symbolic representation of baptism, Jesus Christ speaks about Himself and His action on behalf of the candidate. In baptism He says to the candidate that He also for him and with him is dead and risen and a Partner in the covenant. In baptism He calls and engages man to be what He is in him. In baptism Jesus Christ seals the letter He has written in His Person and with His work and which we by faith in Him have already received. Sealing—*obsignare*—that is the special work of baptism. If it be understood thus, one ought to and must say of it in the words of Scripture : it saves, sanctifies, purifies, mediates and gives the forgiveness of sins and the grace of the Holy Spirit, it effects the new birth, it is the admission of man into the covenant of grace and into the Church. This is all true, so far as it is true, in that an authentic word about it all is decisively said to us in baptism.

For a foreigner to assume the manner, opinions and disposition of a Swiss and the legal act of naturalization by which this is publicly recognised, are clearly two quite different things. Doubtless one who is not " naturalized " in the latter sense, can yet in fact have been long since " *ein guter Schweizer.*" Doubtless also, one who is " naturalized " becomes a Swiss not by means of his citizen's certificate, but in consequence of it; and perhaps in spite of it remains always a pretty poor specimen. But does that mean that for the foreigner and for the Swiss what is carried out in naturalization is an ineffectual and superfluous ceremony? Does not the whole promoting and proving of the foreigner's " Swiss-ness " depend upon it, and therewith for the country the practical possibility of claiming him as a citizen? In the same way baptism is " to be regarded firmly and constantly as a certain sign and witness by the side of the Word, by which the Word is made sure and in which God engages that His promised grace will wash away and blot out our sins."[1] One may gently ask the Romans, the Lutherans and the Anglicans whether and, if so, how far, too little has thereby been said as to the meaning of baptism. But one must also ask them whether there is perhaps some other way in which they intend to venerate the special characteristics of what happens in the sacrament of baptism.

And now in regard to the meaning and work of baptism the following has to be said positively and in particular :—

It is a strange gap in the baptismal teaching of

[1] Luther, *nach Rohrer, Erlangen Ausgabe* 4, 184

all Confessions—the Reformed included—that the meaning and work of baptism have never been understood in principle as a glorifying of God, that is, as a moment in His self-revelation. Perhaps one came near to it when, with Justin, baptism was described as " illumination " (φωτισμός). Justin, indeed, certainly conceived this subjectively; whoever went through the baptismal waters was enlightened. But just because this is true, it should be remembered that, according to Matt. v, 15 and the rest of the New Testament, a lamp kindled by God is not lit for itself but for all who are in the house. Baptism, then, owes its radiance to the *Kabod Jahve*, the δόξα τοῦ θεοῦ, and should in turn serve this. While baptism does its cognitive work, while the divine-human reality illuminates a man, making him an enlightened one, the far greater and primary thing occurs : God receives glory in that He Himself, as man recognises Him in truth, once more secures His just due on earth.

God does this, however, within the framework of the Church of Jesus Christ, when the candidate as a living member of the Church—a lamp kindled in the darkness—is visible to himself and to others. With the exception of Calvin, men have in general concentrated too much on the significance of baptism for the individual. They have given too little prominence to this other side of the matter : that baptism as the sacrament of *regeneratio*[1] is *seminarium civitatis coelestis*, and that this heavenly city like the earthly one needs the natural *generatio*. The Church of Jesus Christ on earth originates, grows and persists through the divine " adding thereto " (Acts ii, 47) of those who, through their baptism

[1] Augustine, *De Civ. Dei* XV, 16, 3

as believers, publicly proclaim themselves as saved and are publicly acknowledged as such. There are of course secret members of the Church of Jesus Christ, not recognised as such by themselves, making no profession, and not acknowledged as such by others. But the Church is not built up by such, either internally or externally. She does not shine in such persons, nor can she in them realise the purpose of her existence, the glorifying of God. On the other hand, every baptism is not only a guarantee of life; it is a proof of life and a functioning of the *ecclesia perpetuo mansura*, a reinforcement of her creed, a public addition to the praise of God for which, from generation to generation, until the Lord comes, the Church is assembled and summoned. The practical liturgical consequence is clear : in principle baptism cannot be celebrated as a private act or a family festival. In principle it can only be celebrated within the framework of the public worship of God.

The central meaning of baptism in its relation to the candidate is now at last clear. With divine certainty there is given to him for the glorifying of God in the upbuilding of the Church of Jesus Christ, the promise that in the death and resurrection of Jesus Christ the grace of God avails for him and is directed to him; that in this happening he also is re-born; that, on the ground of this happening, even he may have assurance of the presence and work of the Holy Spirit; that even his sins are forgiven; that he also is a child of God; that the hope of eternal life is his also. This is the first thing which—not the Church, and not any human being, but the divine human Baptizer Himself has to say and does say to the candidate in this part of the Church's proclamation and through the instrumentality of human words and works. How can He say it except with divine certainty, so that the candidate may hold to it in each and every situation, sure that it is as he has been told? The second thing is this : it has often been improperly pushed into the background, but the meaning of baptism would be imperfectly described, if it were not explicitly mentioned. With divine authority there is pronounced over the candidate, for the glorifying of God in the upbuilding of the Church of Jesus Christ, his pledge of allegiance regarding the grateful service demanded of him. It is said to him that, by virtue of the death and resurrection of Jesus Christ, which happened on his account, he is no longer his own; that he is under obligation to his Deliverer ; that as one who has been certainly and completely freed, he has equally certainly and completely been bound; that he has been set on a path from which henceforth he cannot any more deviate, weak, erring, foolish, wicked though he still is and will be. He has received a Lord. That is the second thing that is said to the candidate in baptism—again by the Baptizer, Jesus Christ Himself—and said as no other but He finally can say it—with divine authority, so that he has no further ground or pretext for disobedience.

That these two things are said to the same person is well understandable. It is of Jesus Christ Himself that we are speaking. As the man to whom this is said is he to whom (Eph. v, 14) Christ has come forth as light, he is intended to serve the divine δόξα instead of his own, and appointed a living member of the Church of Jesus Christ. The experience to which a man is subjected in baptism consists in being made sure with divine certainty and being placed under obligation by divine authority.

IV

THE principles underlying the order *(ordnung)* of baptism are the responsibly undertaken task of the Church on the one side, and on the other the responsible readiness and willingness of the baptized to receive this pledge and to consent to this oath of allegiance.

Baptism is part of the Church's proclamation. But manifestly and inevitably it also concerns the one baptized. Before we speak, as we shall do in the last section, about the effect and result of baptism, obviously we must direct special attention to this aspect of the problem—to the Church which baptizes and to the person who is being baptized.

We have here to do with the question of the ordering and practice of baptism : with baptism, so far distinguished from its nature, potency and meaning as to be seen as a matter of human determination and shaping, from time to time fixed by and dependent upon the order of ecclesiastical judgment and decision. It follows from the nature of the Church as a manifestation of the covenant of grace in the time between the Resurrection and Parousia of Jesus Christ, as indeed it follows from the nature of all the separate parts of the Church's proclamation— baptism among them—that their order and practice as humanly arranged must be kept in mind as a special aspect of the problem as a whole. When the Kingdom of God comes, this distinction will be pointless. Here and now it cannot be escaped. Further, it is true that baptism is given into the hands of men and that the conditions of its administration and reception are matters of human judgment and decision.

At the same time this has certainly to be said : What from this standpoint ought to be or may not be, is or is not, cannot alter in any way or make better or worse what baptism is from the more important standpoint of its divine institution, its divine-human origin, namely, its objective nature, power and meaning. Let us set down at the outset all the things that are here to be held fast : the nature, power and meaning of baptism are fundamentally independent of the order and practice which are mutually conditioned by the Church and the person who is baptized. Let us set down at the outset everything that has here to be said, sued for and demanded, as something half like a precaution : from first principles it is certain that no rejection of the order and practice of baptism through the fault of the Church, or through fault or lack on the part of the candidate, can make the baptism of a person, once it has been performed, ineffective and therefore invalid, or can lead to or justify a call to re-baptism according to a better order and practice.

An inadequate order and practice of baptism can obscure its nature, order, power and meaning, can dull and render difficult the understanding of it. There can be no doubt that this has happened and still happens. The effect of baptism may on that account be subjectively called in question. About this we shall later have something quite definite to say. The paradoxical situation may result that the Church herself does not realise what she is doing in baptism or what she possesses in those who have been baptized. On their side the baptized may not know that they are baptized or what comes to them in the baptism conferred on them by the Church. But there can be no question of any objective destruction of the nature of baptism, any objective annulment of its power, any objective hindering of its work and therefore of any objective ineffectiveness of baptism because of the inadequate administration and inadequate reception of the sacrament. " Gold does not become straw, because a thief steals and misuses it. Silver does not become paper because a usurer acquires it by wrong means."[1] There is no kind of inadequacy in baptismal order and practice that cannot be removed or put right by means quite other than that of re-baptism. That may be written in advance in the remembrance book of Anabaptists of all kinds—Roman and those supposed to be evangelical. Nothing is going to be said here in their favour.

But this again does not mean that there must not be earnest theological consideration of the order and practice of baptism. In this matter also there are principles which cannot be mistaken or neglected without punishment. Their perversion makes possible and actual that obscuring of the content of baptism —invariable though it is in itself—which results in the paradoxical situation of a double uncertainty regarding its effect. The Church in all her branches suffers severely from the fact that, though she certainly has baptism, she has it—as a result of the irregularity of her order—only in the way she has. The question therefore arises, whether the Church could not have baptism in a quite different manner by a better order and practice. The present distress of the Church—often enough bemoaned— may well be connected with the fact that up to now

[1] Luther, *Von der Wiedertaufe*, Weimar Ausgabe 26, 161

36

she has devoted to this question of order all too little attention and willingness to make decisions. Every attempt to rectify this distress may be condemned to failure, if one is unwilling in this matter to seek and then to accept a quite new remedy.

The first foundation principle in the matter of the ordering of baptism lies in the fact that baptism takes place as part of the errand of the Church, responsibly undertaken and accomplished. Baptism, administered by the Church as the carrying out of the command given by Her Lord, with true and careful mindfulness of His will, and with the rite accompanied by the faithful preaching of His word, is true baptism from the point of view of order. One comforted and consoled oneself with a piece of miserable legalism if one let the validity of baptism exhaust itself in the intention of the baptizer, in his pronouncement of the formula of administration which includes the three holy names, or in the wetting of at least the head of the baptized with real water; or when one designated as the normal person to baptize the ordained priest or pastor; or when Romans and Lutherans wanted in cases of emergency to make it incumbent on other persons—even midwives, for example—while, on the contrary, the old Reformers (after the example of Tertullian) got angry only lest some " old women " should have a hand in the game; or when, following the controversy over heretics in the fourth century, one acknowledged heretical baptism if correctly administered, and yet wanted to make certain exceptions among them; or, again, when one invented for doubtful cases the institution of " conditional " baptism[1]; to say nothing of the further hair-splittings of the Roman and

[1] *Si nondum baptizatus es, ego te baptizo.*

unfortunately also the older Protestant dogmatic!

Let this be clearly understood. The painful thing is not that one wanted by such considerations and statements to be in all circumstances punctilious about baptism. That is rather the one thing praiseworthy in such legalism. The painful thing is that thereby, after the manner of the Scribes and Pharisees (Matt. xxiii, 23), mint, anise and cummin are tithed, while the weightier matters of the law—justice, mercy and faith—are left undone. "These ye ought to have done, and not to have left the other undone."

The question of baptism really reaches to the very height and depth of the Church's responsibility. If such cases and conditions were to be brought forward, why have not, *e.g.*, the confession of faith of the baptized, the prayer of the baptizer, the public character of baptism, its relation to the worship of the congregation, also been reckoned among the necessary requisites for its correct performance? Why have men evidently been fixing a minimum instead of a maximum? Why have they obviously aimed at making the road and the door as wide as possible, when in this matter they should plainly be small and narrow? Did not certain basic questions of Tertullian, and even more those of Cyprian—even if one rightly did not wish to accept their practical consequences—deserve more fundamental consideration than has been devoted to them since the victory of the Augustinian solution of the controversy over the heretics? These are some of the questions : By what right is there baptism where a man is not in the one Church, or where the Being of God (and under the three holy Names!) is at least questioned? By what right, where a man cannot be

38

certain of what is laid upon him in baptism? By what right, where a man—openly or secretly, intentionally or in fact—has and professes a faith quite other than that of the New Testament? How can true Christians go forth from the bosom of a false Church? How can there be light in her room, when she herself is in darkness? Would it not be better instead of rejecting the doctrine of Ambrose *Non sanat baptismus perfidorum, non mundat sed polluit* as we have recently done, to listen to it with fear and trembling as a call to unity, a call back to the purity of the one faith, a more constant and on all sides and in every place more valid summons to the renewing of the Church? Can the Church wonder or be offended at those who have been baptized, where she herself, when she baptizes, makes it certainly questionable whether she is the Church and in what sense she must and can become completely new? Can baptism be in order, where concern is absent that before all else the Church needs to put herself in order, and day and night by prayer and service must seek the necessary ways and means? Since she banishes this concern, how can it be otherwise than that she again and again leads the people into the temptation of questioning whether their baptism is in fact the real and effective baptism of Jesus Christ, or whether it must not be restored or replaced by some deplorable sectarian re-baptism? For the clear freedom with which one has since Augustine solved the controversy over the heretics, and for the setting up and carrying through of a pure outward order for baptismal procedure, the Church has the inner right and the spiritual authority in the measure in which she has her affairs in order; but that means in so far as she, conscious of her responsibility all along the line, not only is the Church, but is in process of becoming the Church. Baptism in the Church which is under reformation is genuine baptism.

The second foundation principle in the matter of the ordering of baptism relates to the one baptized. As he is without doubt the second of the chief actors in what takes place, one must ask very seriously about him, too. And one does not ascribe too much to him, nor too little to the irresistible grace of baptism, if one says that—not, indeed, to the nature, power, meaning or effect of baptism, but surely to its order there belongs the following : the responsible willingness and readiness of the baptized person to receive the promise of the grace directed towards him and to be party to the pledge of allegiance concerning the grateful service demanded of him. Only on the basis of a causative or generative understanding of baptism can this second issue regarding order be questioned and, taken literally, then only if one resolves upon the Roman dogmatic, which attributes to the rite of baptism its own effectiveness *ex opere operato*. But it must be pointed out that no one has dared on this ground to evade this particular issue. In no event can this second question of order be neglected from the Reformed standpoint with its cognitive understanding of baptismal grace. Baptism without the willingness and readiness of the baptized is true, effectual and effective baptism, but it is not correct; it is not done in obedience, it is not administered according to proper order, and therefore it is necessarily clouded baptism. It must and ought not to be repeated. It is, however, a wound in the body of the Church and a weakness for the baptized, which can certainly be cured but which are so dangerous that another question presents itself to the Church : how long is she prepared to be guilty of the occasioning of this wounding and weakening through a baptismal practice which is, from this standpoint, arbitrary and despotic?

We have in mind here the custom of the baptism of children, or more exactly the *baptismus infantium* —already acknowledged in the second century according to the witness of Origen[1] and Cyprian[2], become everywhere general since the fourth century, and defended with great energy by all the Reformers. According to the sense of the words this means the baptism of those who before and in the course of what happens have nothing to say; and have nothing to say, because they are not yet able to speak, because one is in consequence not even able to ask what they ought to say, but whom one is wont to baptize with no questions regarding their willingness or their readiness, without making them responsible, in a pure passivity, relying on the fact that they are children of Christian parents. The baptismal teaching prevalent today in all the great Christian Confessions—in the Reformed Church also—has in it at this point not a mere chink but a hole. The baptismal practice found in use on the basis of the prevalent teaching is arbitrary and despotic. Neither by exegesis nor from the nature of the case can it be established that the baptized person can be a merely passive instrument *(Behandelter)*. Rather it may be shown, by exegesis and from the nature of the case, that in this action the baptized is an active partner *(Handelnder)* and that at whatever stage of life he may be, plainly no *infans* can be such a person. We cannot suppress the crucial question

[1] Ep. ad Rom. 5, 9   [2] Ep. 64, 2f.

41

which has here to be put to the Church. We can of course only develop it in outline.[1]

As to exegesis : Baptism is in the New Testament in every case the indispensable answer to an unavoidable question by a man who has come to faith. It answers the question concerning the divine certainty and the divine authority of the word which the man has already heard, which in faith he has already laid hold of and to which he has replied in the affirmative. It answers to his desire for the sealing of his faith and to his acknowledgment of that which he has perceived as the object of his faith. It answers to his wish to be not only inwardly convinced of the fellowship of Jesus Christ with him, but once for all to get a sight of it. It answers him by representing to him a picture of the death and resurrection of Jesus Christ in which he is himself to be seen not as the Chief Actor but certainly as the second, while it portrays before his eyes Jesus Christ as the One crucified for him (Gal. iii, 1). Can the desire for such a happening be wrong? Can this happening itself have any other character than that of an answer to the question of the person baptized?

In the sphere of the New Testament one is not brought to baptism; one comes to baptism. For *infantes, i.e.,* for such as cannot yet let themselves ask or answer—or, to put it another way, for a word of God which in spite of Isaiah lv, 10f., though a forerunner, comes back empty, running on, with-

---

[1] Apart from the literature of the 16. and 17. centuries, one finds detailed (though in result different from what is here propounded) and uncritical considerations on this subject in Schleiermacher, *The Christian Faith,* § 138 and in the writings of Bretschneider, Alex. Schweizer, H. R. Frank, J. A. Dorner, H. H. Wendt, and in the composite volume *Le Baptême* (edited by Jean Cadier), etc.

out accomplishing what it has decreed—we see in the order there followed no room at all; as is indeed seen clearly enough from Acts viii, 28f., x, 44f., xvi, 13f., 32f, xviii, 8f. That Jesus, according to Matt. xix, 13f., let the children be brought to Him, prayed over them, and put His hands on them, and that, according to Matt. xxi, 15f., He finds praise from the mouths of babes and sucklings well-pleasing, is a proof that His kingdom is in fact greater than His Church, but plainly no proof that such children are to be baptized without question.

Further, that the children of Christians are (according to 1 Cor. vii, 14) holy, points again at that wider Kingdom of Christ, but signifies as little that these children are to be baptized as that the same is to be said of the husband sanctified by a believing wife or of a wife sanctified by a believing husband. That the promise, according to Acts ii, 39, holds good for " you and your children " bears witness to its universality in time, just as " baptizing all nations " (Matt. xxviii, 19) witnesses to its universality in space; but not that any of these children were to be drawn into the special, the sacramental grace of baptism—automatically and without having given recognition to their place within it. μαθητεύειν is certainly no action that can be completed without the responsible decision of the one concerned. It is true that baptism is in Colossians ii, 11f. called the circumcision of Christ which we may enter upon instead of the Israelite circumcision, but from this it noways follows that baptism like circumcision is to be carried out on a babe. Circumcision refers to natural birth; it is the sign of the election of the holy lineage of Israel, which with the birth of the Messiah achieved its goal,

43

so that therewith this sign lost its meaning. The succession of those who believed this promise and in this faith were true children of Abraham, was, however, already in pre-messianic Israel (according to Romans iv) in no way identical with the succession of the race and the circumcision of its (male!) members. And so, properly, the succession of those called to the Church of the new covenant (according to John i, 12f.) is plainly not dependent on a racial succession, not on family or nation, but comes in this way: in the life of the individual, now here in this manner, now there in another, there comes an acceptance (λαμβάνειν) of Jesus, a faith in His name. It is this which gives him the power to become a child of God. From the New Testament standpoint it is impossible to say that " everyone who is born of Christian parents is born into the Christian Church *(Gemeinde).*"[1]

If someone recalls, finally, the analogy of vicarious baptism in 1 Cor. xv, 29, what has to be said is that, whatever may be meant by it, the reference is certainly not to a baptism of dead persons who can scarcely transfer their baptism to infants, but only to a baptism for certain dead persons. I know only a thin thread to which one may perhaps hold (and then hardly!) for a proof of infant-baptism from the New Testament: the fact that Acts xvi, 15; xviii, 8 and 1 Cor. i, 16 speak of the baptism of " households " and Acts xvi, 33 of the baptism of οἱ αὐτοὶ of the Philippian jailer, and that these passages do not explicitly forbid the supposition that babies may have been included. One thinks, however, of the sequence that is invariably kept even in these narratives—the preaching of the word, faith,

[1] A. Ritschl, *Unterricht i.d. chr. Rel.,* § 35

44

baptism—and wonders whether one really wants to hold to this thread![1]

Is it not therefore a little arbitrary and a sign of embarrassment when, in face of this circumstance, more than one of the modern defenders of infant baptism assert that one must not understand or use the New Testament " legalistically "? That we certainly do not intend to do. But do not the supporters of infant-baptism with their search for New Testament arguments themselves show that it is not senseless to put the exegetical question first? If one does so, however, one can hardly come to any other conclusion but that the case for a New Testament proof of infant-baptism is more than weak.

The Church which defends infant-baptism, and particularly the Church of the Reformation, is naturally fully conscious of the decisive exegetical problem and has therefore tried again and again to give, above all from the standpoint of her practice, an answer to the question of the relationship in terms of order between baptism and the faith asserted on his own responsibility by the baptized. Here is the essential decisive issue for doctrine : can one be satisfied or not with the different expedients which have been resorted to on this question?

It has been said that babies are baptized on the confession of the faith of the Church or of their parents or god-parents. But is there in this matter of faith any substitution, even the strongest, except that of the faith, which Jesus Christ surely guarantees for us and by which He is ours—but by which, however, He has thereby established our own faith? Luther for a time taught the possibility of such a

[1] On the corresponding practice of the Church of the 2. and 3. centuries compare O. Cullman, *Les premières confessions de foi chrétiennes*, 1943, pp. 15f.

fides aliena, only later to reject it with equal vehemence. In its place he set the idea of a primitive, but at the same time true and real faith, which was to be presupposed in the baptized child himself. Strangely enough, even Calvin[1] knows how to speak of such a seed of future faith and future repentance, brought with him by the child and made active by the Holy Spirit. And J. Wolleb presumed to know : *infantes fidem non secus ac rationem habent; etsi non in fructu, tamen in semine et radice: etsi non in actu secundo, tamen actu primo; etsi non operis externa demonstratione, tamen Spiritus sancti interna virtute.*[2] In distinction therefrom, the later Lutherans taught that the faith of the child is first imparted through baptism together with regeneration. Since at the same time they held fast to the view that faith and the confession of faith, prior to baptism, is to be required of adults (converted Jews perhaps), they came to the strange position that baptism effects something quite different in children and in adults. In children it effects regeneration and faith, and to that end a ratification of their justification before God, which is to be made fruitful in riper years; but in adults, after they have already received the new birth and faith through the word of God and prior to baptism, simply (suddenly according to Reformed teaching !) an *obsignatio et testificatio de gratia Dei* and thereby an increase of their renewal and of the gift of the Holy Spirit.[3] But no one is able to specify as to how precisely one should conceive this *fides infantilis,* which is presupposed

[1] *Institutes* IV 16, 20
[2] *Comp. chr. Theol.,* 1626, I, 23, 15
[3] Is it clear in present day missionary work, where there seems to be agreement in a double practice of baptism, that such presupposes a double teaching regarding the meaning of baptism?

and which is to be made effective through baptism. And one may surely say with truth that it asks too much to refer to such a hazardous possibility—or rather one invented in such notorious embarrassment —rather than depending on the due reverence of faith before the secrets of God. One is led by this hypothesis out of one maze into another. But a satisfactory defence of infant-baptism cannot be given with the help of this hypothesis, even if in itself it could be carried through. For what would be lacking to such an unconscious faith (*Kinderglaube*) if one had to reckon with it, is the possibility of its confession and of the request for baptism; and plainly to ask after that must not be omitted, if baptism is to avoid the character of an act of violence. The judicious Calvin therefore made only the most sparing use of this hypothesis and instead[1] understood the decisive faith of the baptized child to be that which has to be authenticated and confessed in later life.

This is the interpretation of infant-baptism which one may describe as most frequently held today. But even this has had added to it the necessity of so-called Confirmation—" the ratification of the baptismal covenant." One cannot deny that infant-baptism calls aloud for such a completion and supplementing. Schleiermacher says with simple truth : " Infant Baptism is a complete Baptism only when the profession of faith which comes after further instruction is regarded as the act which consummates it."[2] But what is baptism in itself and as such, if it has no reference to the conscious acknowledgment of regeneration and faith, to the complete divine-human reality, which is portrayed within it; if it cannot be

[1] *Institutes* IV 16, 21-22
[2] *Der Christliche Glaube* § 138; E.T. p. 633

in a really intelligible sense the confirming and bind-
ing in allegiance of the second of the chief actors,
the one baptized; if it cannot be a matter of decision
and confession at all? Is it in this case full baptism?
Is it not rather, and notoriously, half-baptism? And,
on the other hand, what right have we to attribute
to confirmation the significance of a half-sacrament?
Can it be more than admission to the Lord's Supper,
the climax of the instruction given by the Church?

Calvin rightly called the very name *confirmatio*
an *iniuria baptismi.*[1] But on the supposition of
infant-baptism, one ought not to talk so openly of
the abolition or making harmless of confirmation.
For where will then be that other half of the sacrament of baptism which is lacking in infant-baptism?
Is there not, however, perhaps an *iniuria* done to it
here? According to Calvin's own and in itself excell-
ent baptismal teaching, baptism consists not only in
our receiving the symbol of grace, but[2] it is at the
same time, in our *consentire cum omnibus christianis,*
in our public *affirmare* of our faith, in our *iurare* in
God's name, also the expression of a human *velle.*
This without doubt it must be, in virtue of the cognitive character of the sacramental power. But then,
in that case, baptism can be no kind of infant-
baptism. How strange that Calvin seems to have
forgotten this in his next chapter where he sets out
his defence of infant-baptism, there commending a
baptism which is without decision and confession!
Must that *consentire, affirmare, iurare* be at some
time filled out in order to make baptism complete?

The statement may be hazarded that the confusion, with which Luther and Calvin and their

[1] *Institutes* IV 19, 13
[2] *Institutes* IV 15, 13

followers on both sides have thrown themselves in this matter, is hopeless. One has to admit that—unlike the moderns—they gave themselves really fiercely to the answering of this burning doctrinal question. But it still has to be said that the actual information which one gets from them on the decisive point is, in fact, as incredible as its exegetical grounds are unsatisfactory. One may read the 15th and 16th chapters in Book IV of the *Institutio* one after the other and convince oneself where the great Calvin was sure of his subject and where he obviously was not sure, but visibly nervous, in a hopelessly confused train of thought, abusing where he ought to inform and when he wants to convince, seeking a way in the fog, which can lead him to no goal, because he has none.

From the standpoint of a doctrine of baptism, infant-baptism can hardly be preserved without exegetical and practical artifices and sophisms—the proof to the contrary has yet to be supplied! One wants to preserve it only if one is resolved to do so on grounds which lie outside the biblical passages on baptism and outside the thing itself. The determination to defend it on extraneous grounds has certainly found expression from century to century.

Let us quickly set down the extraneous reasons which are said to be important.

Calvin[1] in really affecting fashion referred to the need which pious parents have of comfort, as making infant-baptism desirable, and the same argument is put forward today from the mission fields. It is a humanly understandable and respectable point of view. But with what justice is baptism laid claim to for the satisfaction of this need—and a baptism with

[1] *Institutes* IV 16, 9 and 32

its true order distorted? In the time elapsing between the Resurrection and the Parousia of Jesus the relationship between parents and children can no longer have the decisive significance which it had for pre-messianic Israel. It certainly has not the right to make of ecclesiastical order open disorder. Ought not the parents to be informed without this disorder? Can they not be told that they do not need to mourn, that their infant children are in the Kingdom of Christ?

Calvin, again,[1] understood infant-baptism inversely as instituted for the welfare and benefit of the child, obliging the parents, the god-parents and the whole community to give him a Christian up-bringing. There must be mention of this justifiable solicitude in our baptismal liturgies, which are governed by practical considerations, and certainly there is much new wine to be put into the old skins in order to inculcate such seriousness. But here also it has to be asked whether for the proclamation of this earnest solicitude baptism should be brought into service—and a baptism with its true order distorted? Christian baptism, so far as it means obligation, means that of the baptized himself and not that of any one else. If there were need of a rite for laying obligation on others—but is there?—it could be just as well expressed in some sort of public presentation and blessing *(présentation)* of the new-born child.

Today many are supporters of infant-baptism because they are afraid of all kinds of " dangers " from one of the forms of baptism which presupposes free decision and a confession by the baptized, and which thus takes the place of present-day confirmation—dangers such as an unhealthy forcing of

[1] *Institutes* IV 16, 9

conversions, scrupulosity, false illusions of sanctity, the rise of pharisaic " churches of the élite " (*Kerngemeinde*), and so on. To this it must be answered that— here as elsewhere—" dangers " are no reason against recognising and doing what is right. Good baptismal instruction, indeed, would not necessarily prove impotent in the face of such " dangers." The real question in a baptism marked by willingness and preparedness is not the separation, before the appointed time, of the sheep from the goats, believers from unbelievers, the righteous from the unrighteous, the true Body of Christ from nominal Christians who give lip-service only. It is something quite different, and it is this : to give opportunity once more for the free movement and control of the Holy Spirit in the calling and assembling of the Church, to which the present-day baptismal practice tries to do grievous violence. Without any legalism, it would easily be possible so to shape baptismal practice that the baptizing Church assured herself—not with regard to the faith, regeneration, conversion, endowment with the Spirit of those she baptizes, but of their free resolve and confession; so that the baptized might always remember their baptism as an experience in which they were participating in their own persons, by the consequences of which they ought to and must be affected, by which they are singled out from the Church and from everyone else before the whole world. Is not the real " danger," the existence of a Christendom, which, even in matters affecting Christianity itself, can with a certain formal justice disclaim responsibility, though this is still so hidden from us that we can afford to argue about these other dangers? Is " Perfectionism " really our greatest concern?

Many good theologians would today part reluctantly with infant-baptism because undoubtedly it offers a very drastic illustration of the Reformation teaching of the free antecedent grace of God. That is certainly true. It is indeed remarkable that the Reformers themselves, so far as I can see, made hardly any use of this argument. One must treat the matter with a certain caution. With the summary explanation that the truth of God ought not to be made dependent on our faith, one might justify a practice like that which Charlemagne employed with the Saxons, or that at one time used by Roman Catholic missionaries in South America, when they baptized whole villages of Indians with a kind of fireman's syringe. It must also not be overlooked that from this argument a claim might be put forward for the admission of infants to the Lord's Supper. Indeed, since by reason of their baptism they are members of the Church, properly speaking this must be claimed. Seriously, this argument from antecedent grace would carry weight only if the rightness of infant-baptism could have been proved in some other way. The teaching about free grace can be illustrated, if not so drastically, yet more completely and exactly, in free and responsible baptism.

Am I wrong in thinking that the really operative extraneous ground for infant-baptism, even with the Reformers, and ever and again quite plainly since, has been this : one did not want then in any case or at any price to deny the existence of the evangelical Church in the Constantinian *corpus christianum*— and today one does not want to renounce the present form of the national church *(Volkskirche)*? If she were to break with infant-baptism, the Church would not easily any longer be a people's church in the sense of a state Church or a church of the masses. *Hinc, hinc illae lacrymae!* Has not the anxiety, which here shows itself, often unconsciously the quite primitive form to which Luther openly confessed on occasion : there would not be too many people baptized, if, instead of being brought to baptism, they had to come of their own accord? We make no mistake about the difficulty of personal decision—historical, practical and actual—which is here indeed obvious. But in spite of it we may ask : are these legitimate anxieties? Would it not always turn out even in this matter that to be successful in what one intends, in any case and at whatever price, one must examine it closely? Are we so sure of the inner worth of the Constantinian system and of the present day form of the National Church—is our conscience in these matters so clear—that we ought and must resolve to hold fast to them, at whatever cost—even at the cost of inflicting wounds and weakness on the Church through a disorderly baptism? Or, on the contrary, does not the unmistakable disorder of our baptismal practice show at once just this : that there is a disorder in the sociological structure of our Church, which perhaps must still be endured for a long time, but which can in no case be cited as a serious argument against the better ordering of our baptismal practice? Where does it stand written that Christians may not be in the minority, perhaps in a very small minority? Might they not be of more use to their surroundings, if they were allowed to be a healthy Church? What is really wanted for the Church to remain a National Church in the present-day sense of the term : a Church *of* the people, instead of a Church *for* the people? Theology has to state that the pressing issue of a better ordering of

53

our baptismal practice is relevant to the question how that may come about.

This it is then that has to be said concerning the order of baptism from the standpoint of the candidate : there is a call for reinstatement. What is wanted is very simple : instead of the present infant-baptism, a baptism which on the part of the baptized is a responsible act. If it is to be natural, the candidate, instead of being a passive object of baptism, must become once more the free partner of Jesus Christ, that is, freely deciding, freely confessing, declaring on his part his willingness and readiness.

[The question as to how this reinstatement is to come about in practice does not really belong to the sphere of this doctrinal presentation. I have my own views on the matter and intended to give them expression in my lecture at Gwatt for the sake of completeness. The relevant passage is here suppressed because I wanted readers to give their attention firstly and exclusively to the theological question —undisturbed by considerations of ecclesiastical politics—and to measure my statement by theological standards. All that has to happen must begin in any case with a fresh taking up of the theological consideration of this special point of baptismal doctrine, and that unfortunately has not been done since the 16th century. But those who are intimately concerned with, interested in and appointed to ecclesiastical politics may not escape the responsibility, by supposing it shifted on to others, or avoid considering the matter from their standpoint.]

V.

THE efficacy of baptism consists in this, that the baptized person is placed once and for all under the sign of hope, in consequence of which he has death already behind him and only life in front of him, and in consequence of which his light will shine to the glory of God among the peoples, because his sins are forgiven.

Let us turn back to our starting-point in Thesis I. What happens to a man in baptism is that he is placed and places himself in the darkness and the light of this fact : that in the death and resurrection of Jesus Christ he also is dead and risen again. In baptism he is convinced of this with divine certainty and may assure himself of it; he is thereby bound by divine authority and he engages himself thereto. " For ye are all sons of God, through faith, in Christ Jesus. For as many of you as were baptized into Christ did put on Christ " (Gal. iii, 26-27). In the promise made us by God in baptism that which is promised is itself abundantly present, as Gregory of Nyssa[1] explicitly expressed it. Your baptism is your *tota innocentia, tota pietas, tota gratia, tota sanctificatio;* so Ambrose[2] charged the candidates. " Baptism makes a man once for all and completely pure and blessed, so that there is nothing lacking for the title or heritage of blessedness than such faith in the mercy of such a God."[3]

" Through baptism, once we receive it, we are laid hold of and taken into the number of those who are to be blessed and God makes with us an everlasting

[1] *Or. Cat.* 33 [2] *De Sacram.* I, 13, 10
[3] Luther, *Weimar Ausgabe* 10, I, 112

covenant of grace."[1] "Christ by baptism has made us partakers of His death . . . and those who receive baptism with true faith truly feel *(vere sentiunt)* the efficacy of Christ's death in the mortification of their flesh and the efficacy of His resurrection in the quickening of the Spirit."[2] If we read these and similar strong, triumphant words from the New Testament, the Early Church and the Reformers, concerning the effect of baptism on the baptized, and are inclined to ask whether they do not say too much, whether "magical" ideas—from which we have so laudably freed ourselves—have not an unlawful place in them, then this has to be remembered : these and all such words say too little rather than too much. No Christian is so good a Christian that his understanding and experience of the fulness of the grace that is his in baptism could correspond other than distantly to the reality. Moreover, how greatly baptism is everywhere obscured for us by the various disfigurements and perversions in its observance! How far removed from us in practice is the power to form a clear judgment in this matter! Once one sees even for a moment through all the confusion for which one is personally responsible and through all the practical order and disorder in regard to baptism, its true nature, power and meaning, then one must admit that concerning its effect—concerning what it in fact performs—one cannot think highly enough, or speak strongly enough.

Let us once more be quite clear that no abuse of baptism can affect in any way its actual efficacy. It is independent of the purity or impurity, the worthiness or unworthiness, of the church which administers

[1] Luther, *Weimar Ausgabe* 37, 668
[2] Calvin, *Institutes* IV 15, 5

it or of her representatives. *Non recte datur, tamen datur,* wrote Augustine,[1] concerning heretical baptism. *Corrigo in te, quod tuum est, agnosco quod Christi est.*[2] " If I should wait till I am certain that the one who baptizes is holy, then neither I nor anyone else would ever be baptized and I should have to expunge from the Lord's Prayer that we must all say : Forgive us our trespasses !"[3] " Be it that those who baptized us were most ignorant of God and all piety, or were despisers, still they did not baptize us into a fellowship with their ignorance or sacrilege, but into the faith of Jesus Christ . . . Our baptism was of God and included in it the promise of forgiveness of sin."[4] Convictions of this kind were the result of the conflict with the heretics of the fourth century, behind which one need not again go back. There may be border-line cases in which it is impossible in practice to recognise as such what is called the act of baptism. But it is well in this matter to allow the poor, baptizing Church in all her forms the advantage of too much rather than too little.

What baptism effects, can manifestly, in the nature of the case, not be dependent—so far as it takes and concerns the candidate—either on the quantity of piety or impiety with which he receives the sacrament, or on the Christian perfection or imperfection with which he afterwards, as receiver of the sacrament, sets to work and proves himself. Here also there comes in question a perfect sea of abuse of baptism, a perfect abyss of denial and treachery. The efficacy of baptism can obviously be darkened by such personal misuse by the candidate,

[1] *De bapt.*, I, 1, 2
[2] *De unico bapt.* 2, 3
[3] Luther, *Weimar Ausgabe* 37, 665
[4] Calvin, *Institutes* IV 15, 16

so that it becomes to him an almost or even completely unknown thing. One must, however, say, with the baptismal teaching of the Reformers, that baptism can no more be annulled by this than by ecclesiastical misuse. It operates irresistibly : *ad dandam gratiam non modo non ponentibus, set etiam obstinatissime ponentibus obicem.*[1]

The Roman Church has made baptism practically meaningless, by reckoning with the possibility of an *obex* (obstacle), which can be opposed to baptismal grace, by the baptized person himself; by describing this grace as a thing which can be terribly easily and quickly lost through new sins beginning after baptism; and by placing behind baptism the much more easily handled sacrament of penance, for the putting right of such loss. And it is indeed noteworthy that the Roman Christian, although he is taught that baptism was absolutely necessary for him and that through it *ex opere operato* there has come to him forgiveness of sins and regeneration, up to the present day has from his baptism (inalienable and needing no completing) no more than the imparting of a Christian " character," indestructible but entirely empty of content, the prerequisite for the reception of the six remaining sacraments. Through the possession of this " disposition " he can as well believe as not believe, as well be saved as lost. The mountain has brought forth a mouse. Fortunately, however, this is how it stands for the Roman Christian only according to the text of his dogmatic. " For what God creates and effects are works that are steadfast, certain, unchangeable and eternal, just as He is unchangeable and eternal. Therefore they endure and remain steadfast and unmoved and are not

[1] Luther, *De capt. Babyl.*

58

altered even if one misuses them altogether. But what *we* do is unstable and uncertain, as we ourselves are, so that one can neither rest nor build upon it . . . That I have been baptized is not my work, nor is that which it has given to me. For it is called not my baptism, nor that of the priest or any other person, but the baptism of Christ, my Lord, and it needs nothing at all of the purity of either me or you. For neither I nor anyone else can hallow baptism and make it pure, but all of us must be hallowed and made pure by baptism."[1] The whole argument of Paul in Rom. vi, Gal. iii and Col. ii would be sophistic rhetoric, if he had not reckoned that in all circumstances baptism has for the baptized a real significance, an absolute efficacy—that is, one in no way consisting simply of a shadowy " character," but an efficacy which because of its nature, its power and its meaning laughs at any *obex*. Good heavens, who dare boast over against the grace that is his in baptism of anything more than being the only and indeed formidable *obex?*

The baptized man differs from the unbaptized in all circumstances as one who has been placed under the sign of the death and resurrection of Jesus Christ, under the sign of His hope, His destiny, His advent, because of the divine decree accepted and expressed over him. He differs from the unbaptized in all circumstances; whether he reflects upon it or not, whether he takes notice of it or not, whether he does it honour or not, he is by that sign a designated man, by that representation a man who has been thereby conditioned. This is not of his own making; nor can he cease to be such of his own accord. He can put an end to the life given him by God. He

[1] Luther, *Weimar Ausgabe*, 37, 665, 666

cannot divest himself of his baptism, just as no one else can take it from him. He may become a Mohammedium, aesthete or atheist, a National Socialist or a Bolshevik, or—worst of all—a heretic, or a bad or a merely nominal Christian. He may become a Catholic. He does not however cease to stand under the sign. The whole teeming, evil humanity of western lands stands under the sign. It may—in the patience and wrath of God—have come *per nefas* far in that direction, and there is the probability—this also in the patience and wrath of God—that it may make a correspondingly fatal use of it. But that humanity does stand under the sign is no less true, and perhaps—no, certainly—this is the best that can be said of it. Both Hitler and Stalin, both Mussolini and the Pope stand under the sign. For the right understanding of this matter by the most devout Christian, as well as the one of ripest perception and decision, everything may depend on the fact that he himself—remembering his own waywardness—is not ashamed to stand under this sign, together with all kinds of wayward and most strange people. There are in the acknowledgment of this sign, in its observance, in its use, in the human attitude taken towards it and, connected therewith, in the form of faith and life which result, great, tremendously great, differences. One will be best employed in clearing the circumference of his own faith and life, not that of others. The very sign, however, as such, stands and remains and has its significance for all these men; let each one again think first and above everything of what he himself would do if this sign—in spite of all changes and hesitations—had not been created for him. He will certainly then not deny that the same holds also for others, and for the most desperate cases among these others, and that it is to their advantage, as it is to his own.

One should not despise this sign because it is in itself so insignificant; because its mark—unlike that of the circumcision of the Israelites—cannot afterwards be seen; because the few drops of water, with which we were once sprinkled with the invocation of the Trinity, dried up long ago; because it consists now only in the fact that this rite was performed once upon a time in our lives, whereof—according to present baptismal practice—we have no recollection at all, but simply a certificate. It was, however, an actual occurrence; it was, however, this representation that took place and we ourselves were in the centre of it. And this representation, in the centre of which we were, was the representation of Good Friday and of Easter Day as the evening and the morning of the great day of our lives. It is apparently insignificant, but it is not to be revoked and there is nothing to be changed so far as its meaning is concerned. In the same way, one may and should think of the baptism of every other person. How else may a man think rightly of his own baptism?

Nor should we despise this sign because, maybe, there have occurred between the day of our baptism and the present time many happenings, encounters, and experiences, spiritual illuminations and moral advances, which may seem to us much more important and impressive signs of our fellowship with God. Let it be noted which sign it is that carries us victoriously through everything, through the less edifying experiences of our lives as well as those which cut into them more deeply! It is related of Luther that he had hours during which he was confused about everything—about the Reformation, about his faith, even

61

about the work of Jesus Christ Himself,—hours when he knew of nothing else to help him (and help him it did) save the writing in chalk on his table of the two words : *Baptizatus sum!* A magical conception? At any rate, a strangely sober magic, which knows how to work with such a simple reminder, and to work so effectively! But he who knows how to comfort himself thus, will not dispute that the same comfort is really available for others, who at present perhaps seem ignorant of it, who perhaps never will know of it.

Let us now try to describe in as few words as possible the essence of this sign, valid and efficacious in its full significance for every baptized person. It is the sign of hope, granted by the Church as part of its service to the baptized, as certainly as it is the sign of Jesus Christ (of the death which He once experienced and of the resurrection of His complete body which also He once experienced) and also the sign of the individual in question. It is therefore an eschatological sign. That is to say : the appearance of the reality which it denotes will occur in and with the appearance of Jesus Christ as the goal and end of the period begun with His resurrection. It designates the baptized as one who, although he still lives, has his death already behind him because of the death of Jesus Christ on his behalf; as one who, because of the resurrection of Jesus Christ on his behalf, although he must die, has in front of him his real life, eternal life in the new Age of the coming Kingdom—and this life only. Precisely as an eschatological sign, it points also into the heart of the life which the baptized is living here and now; to his past, and to his future at the time of that Aeon, which is present with us and hastening towards its goal and end. It points to his past here and now; that is, however, to the forgiveness of his sins, which has happened in Jesus Christ. And it points to his future here and now; that is, however, to his intention to shine to the glory of God as one who has been forgiven out of free compassion. There is no other past and no other future beneath this sign. This and nothing else is truly signified by this sign for time and eternity for the baptized person. He who has received this sign is appointed and furnished for the glorifying of God in the upbuilding of the Church of Jesus Christ, for witnessing to the coming reign of God. There is nothing to object to if one wants to regard him as in fact the bearer of a *character indelebilis*. Such a character must then be understood, however, not as an empty mould, but as the intention and equipment imparted to the baptized in all their rich content. It is really something indestructible, which he can call upon in all circumstances and to which in all circumstances he may hold.

Granted, this sign must be apprehended and taken hold of ever and again by faith. Granted—the great warning of 1 Cor. x, 1-13 must never be forgotten! —it avails a man nothing, if this does not happen. But, if this does happen, to every baptized person it cannot be said too emphatically that the sign has been given to him, it cannot be taken again and he can reject faith only by senseless contradiction of this sign. Granted, there must be life corresponding to this sign. But this is not the most important thing on which to insist. Rather this : that the person bound under this sign is engaged to a life of responsibility. Granted, even under this sign one may fail, fall and sink. But this is not the thing which it is most necessary everyone should hear.

Rather this : that the sign never ceases to be a summons directed to all who are failing, falling and sinking—and which of us is not? Granted, under this sign there is still trouble, shame, judgment and the burning wrath of God. But this is not the essential thing which has to be said about it. Rather this : that, whether recognised or not, it is unalterably the sign of comfort and warning, the sign of promise. One can address a person from many different points of view; but if one addresses him concerning God's eternal election and concerning its consequence that Jesus Christ died and rose again for him and concerning the citizenship he received at his baptism, then one presupposes that the promise holds good for him and continues sure.

Just because of this its finally valid efficacy, baptism needs neither repetition nor over-emphasis. Just because of this any arbitrary re-baptism involves a defaming of baptism and is, as Vilmar[1] has rightly said, blasphemy against God. The Lord's Supper, preaching, and prayer may and should be repeated. The praise of God is the theme of each new day, each new hour. The glory of baptism among all the parts of the Church's proclamation is its "once-for-all-ness." For Jesus Christ died once for our sins and awakened once from the dead for our justification : ἐφάπαξ, once for all.

[1] *Dogmatik*, 1874, II, p. 241